# 100
# Ways to Overcome
# Depression

# 100
# Ways to Overcome
# Depression

Frank B. Minirth
States V. Skipper
Paul D. Meier

**SPIRE**

## TO OUR CHILDREN

Rachel Minirth

Renee Minirth

Carrie Minirth

Todd Skipper

Amy Skipper

Dan Meier

Cheryl Meier

Mark Meier

Beth Ann Meier

# FOREWORD

"We aren't what we think we are—but we are what we think." One way to change our feelings is to change our thoughts.

In this little book, you will find some sweet truths from the book of God to suck on. Wise is the man or woman who in the midst of a midnight of life meditates on them day and night.

*Haddon Robinson*

Department Chairman and
Professor of Pastoral Ministries
Dallas Theological Seminary

# CONTENTS

# PART ONE

## Developing a Better Relationship with God

# 1

## Draw Close to God

*For the eyes of the Lord run to and fro throughout the whole earth, to show himself strong in the behalf of them whose heart is perfect toward him*

(II Chron. 16:9a).

---

The depressed person longs to be close to someone. In this verse, God states that He is looking for people who want to know Him. God longs to be close to us! People frequently feel that in spite of their efforts they can't get close to God. In childhood, they may have failed in their attempts to become intimate with their earthly father. They assume that God is a heavenly version of their earthly father. They wrongly transfer their feelings of being rejected by their earthly father to feelings of being rejected by their heavenly Father. This passage of Scripture shows us that, in reality, God is yearning for intimacy with us and even looking to and fro throughout the whole earth for those who are willing to accept intimacy with Him. He longs to show us how strong He can be in our lives if our hearts (mind, emotions, and will) are perfectly yielded to Him.

# 2

### Draw Close to God

*As the hart panteth after the water brooks, so
panteth my soul after thee, O God* (Ps. 42:1).

---

Some of the most godly men through the ages have
suffered from depression. A list of these men would
include Elijah, David, and from more recent times,
Martin Luther. They all resolved their inner emptiness through a close walk with God.

# 3

## Draw Close to God

*Whom have I in heaven but thee? and there is none upon earth that I desire beside thee. My flesh and my heart faileth: but God is the strength of my heart, and my portion for ever* (Ps. 73: 25, 26).

---

It is natural for all of us at one time or another to experience problems. There are times when our physical and emotional capabilities do not sufficiently cope with every problem. During these times God wants to show me His great strength. Acknowledging Him as "the strength of my heart," as David did in this psalm, I know I can depend on Him. The heart is the seat of the mind, emotions, and will. If I turn my heart over to God, He will be "my portion for ever."

# 4

## Draw Close to God

*Thou wilt keep him in perfect peace, whose mind is stayed on thee: because he trusteth in thee* (Isa. 26:3).

---

A lack of internal peace characterizes the depressed person. One way for him to gain this peace is to "stay" his mind on God. Anxiety is really lack of faith. It is a fear of the unknown. It is frequently a fear of finding out the truth about our own unconscious motives, desires, and temptations. If we really trust and depend on God, He will relieve our fears of the unknown; if we draw close to Him, we can depend upon Him to love us in spite of our faults and to help us to gradually overcome them. We will thus become more and more like His Son, Jesus Christ. We will be participating in His sanctification of us, and our minds will be kept, by Him, "in perfect peace."

# 5

## Draw Close to God

*O Jerusalem, Jerusalem, thou that killest the prophets, and stonest them which are sent unto thee, how often would I have gathered thy children together, even as a hen gathereth her chickens under her wings, and ye would not!* (Matt. 23:37).

---

One of the keys to dealing with our various emotional states is to recognize that Christ really is for us, that He wants to see us find happiness in life. If we recognize this, we are freed to open ourselves to the good things He has for us.

During a hailstorm, a mother hen—at the risk of her own life—instinctively opens her wings for her young chicks to run under, in order to save their lives. In this precious passage of Scripture, Christ shows His tremendous love for us humans by alluding to his own approaching death on the cross for our sins, comparing it indirectly to a mother hen gathering her chicks under her wings to protect them. Surely Christ stands ready to love us and protect us if only we will let Him. He gives us that choice. The Jews He witnessed to in Jerusalem that day chose to reject Him, but we (whether we are Gentile or Jewish) can choose to accept His intimacy and His protection from etenal damnation as well as from the hell of emotional pain in this life.

# 6

## Draw Close to God

*For ye have not received the spirit of bondage again to fear; but ye have received the Spirit of adoption, whereby we cry, Abba, Father* (Rom. 8:15).

---

The depressed person feels as though he is in bondage. He is in bondage to his depression. God has reminded us that He is our Father, and He wants us to talk with Him about our fears. To some extent our parents may have accepted us conditionally. We may, at times, have feared their rejection if we did not live up to their expectations. In that sense, we were in bondage to them. Their rejections lowered our own self-esteem. Our heavenly Father, on the other hand, is perfectly loving. If we have received His Son, Jesus Christ, as our personal Savior, then we are adopted into His eternal family. He accepts us *unconditionally*, as only God can; and we are no longer under a "spirit of bondage again to fear," as we were with our imperfect human parents.

# 7

## Draw Close to God

*He that spared not his own Son, but delivered him up for us all, how shall he not with him also freely give us all things?* (Rom. 8:32).

---

Persons who have had a lifelong habit of handling their problems by becoming depressed, angry, or worried need to learn more satisfactory and effective ways of handling their problems. It is helpful to recognize that our heavenly Father, who was willing to spare His own Son's life for us, stands willing and ready to give us "all things." The phrase "all things" can definitely include eventual victory over a depressive life-style. The fruits of drawing close to God and yielding to His Spirit are love, joy, and peace; they replace our human tendency toward bitterness, depression, and anxiety.

# 8

### Trust God

*Is any thing too hard for the Lord?* (Gen. 18:14a).

---

When individuals say, "I can't," what they usually mean is, "I won't." When anyone says he *can't* get over his depression, he might well encourage himself by recalling this rhetorical question which God asked of Abraham. For the Christian, there is no such thing as "can't." The Christian can do all things, including getting over a period of depression, through Christ who strengthens him. Nothing is too hard for the Lord!

# 9

## Trust God

*God is not a man, that he should lie; neither the son of man, that he should repent: hath he said, and shall he not do it? or hath he spoken, and shall he not make it good?* (Num. 23:19).

When a person becomes depressed he often finds it difficult to believe that anyone is genuinely interested in him. One's confidence in others (including God) often becomes shaken. God wants to reassure us that He is actively at work in our lives even though we may not be aware of His faithfulness to us. He won't lie to us. He will make His promises good. But many chronically depressed Christians fail to responsibly handle their internalized anger and refuse to do what they need to do to get over their depression. They blame God for not making their depression disappear, though in reality the responsibility is their own.

# 10

### Trust God

*The Lord is my shepherd; I shall not want. He maketh me to lie down in green pastures: he leadeth me beside the still waters. He restoreth my soul*

(Ps. 23:1-3a).

---

This is one of the most quoted passages in the Bible. God has used it through the centuries to comfort many hearts, to restore many souls. If I will trust God, He will shepherd me, lead me beside still waters, and restore my soul. What a tremendous comfort!

# 11

## Trust God

*I had fainted, unless I had believed to see the good-ness of the Lord in the land of the living. Wait on the Lord: be of good courage, and he shall strengthen thine heart: wait, I say, on the Lord* (Ps. 27:13, 14).

---

One of the ways that we can wholesomely deal with the various traumas that we experience in life (including depression) is to actively expect that God will do for us that which He has said He will do. In this verse God promises that in time He will strengthen our hearts (minds, emotions, and will).

# 12

## Trust God

*The steps of a good man are ordered by the Lord: and he delighteth in his way. Though he fall, he shall not be utterly cast down: for the Lord upholdeth him with his hand* (Ps. 37:23, 24).

---

God does watch out for His children. He loves us beyond what we can comprehend. We can understand His love to some degree by considering how much we love our children. He is very concerned when we fall. He wants to help us up. He will protect us if only we will trust Him to order our steps.

# 13

### Trust God

*He brought me up also out of an horrible pit, out of the miry clay, and set my feet upon a rock, and established my goings* (Ps. 40:2).

---

God can bring us out of the horrible pit of depression. He can give us stability. He can set our feet on solid rock. He can help us establish a behavior pattern (our "goings") that will bring us joy. If we *do* what God wants us to do, we will *feel* the way God wants us to feel.

# 14

## Trust God

*Do you not know? Have you not heard?*
*The Everlasting God, the Lord, the creator of the*
*ends of the earth*
*Does not become weary or tired.*
*His understanding is inscrutable.*
*He gives strength to the weary,*
*And to him who lacks might He increases power.*
*Though youths grow weary and tired,*
*And vigorous young men stumble badly,*
*Yet those who wait for the Lord*
*Will gain new strength;*
*They will mount up with wings like eagles,*
*They will run and not get tired,*
*They will walk and not become weary.*

(Isa. 40:28-31, NASB)

---

When we are depressed we become weary and tired, and may even stumble more. But God never wearies or tires. He desires to give us strength and to encourage us. He understands what we are going through. He sees through us and perceives even our unconscious and subconscious motives. He wants us to *take up His strength in place of our weakness*. He wants us to wait for (depend on) Him to give us the strength to do what He wants us to do.

# 15

### Trust God

*But now thus saith the Lord that created thee, O Jacob, and he that formed thee, O Israel, Fear not: for I have redeemed thee, I have called thee by thy name; thou art mine. When thou passest through the waters, I will be with thee; and through the rivers, they shall not overflow thee; when thou walkest through the fire, thou shalt not be burned; neither shall the flame kindle upon thee (Isa. 43:1, 2).*

---

If we have accepted Christ as our Savior, then we belong to God. What God said years ago to the children of Israel, He says to us today, "Thou art mine." He will be with us when we pass through the waters—the rivers will not overflow us.

# 16

### Trust God

*And the Lord shall guide thee continually, and satisfy thy soul in drought, and make fat thy bones: and thou shalt be like a watered garden, and like a spring of water, whose waters fail not* (Isa. 58:11).

---

God promised the children of Israel that He would satisfy their "soul in drought." He can satisfy our soul today when we are in the drought of depression. He can make us like a well-watered garden or a perennial spring of water.

# 17

### Trust God

*For I know the thoughts that I think toward you,
saith the Lord, thoughts of peace, and not of evil, to
give you an expected end* (Jer. 29:11).

---

In this verse God was speaking to His children
(Israel) while they were captives in Babylon. Today,
He can encourage us when we are captives of depression. We can be assured that He wants us to experience an abundant life of joy and peace.

# 18

### Trust God

*For, behold, I am for you, and I will turn unto you, and ye shall be tilled and sown* (Ezek. 36:9).

---

Feelings of hopelessness and helplessness often pervade the life of the depressed person. The depressed person can be encouraged if he will notice in the Scriptures the numerous times that God has helped those who have felt hopeless and helpless.

# 19

## Trust God

*The Lord is good, a strong hold in the day of trouble; and he knoweth them that trust in him* (Nah. 1:7).

---

A strong need for security generally pervades the life of man. Depression often erodes our security. In this verse, God offers to be our strong hold—our security—if we put our trust in Him.

# 20

### Trust God

*Not by might, nor by power, but by my spirit, saith the Lord of hosts* (Zech. 4:6b).

---

When one feels that a depression is beyond what he can overcome, he needs to realize that God can overcome anything. No man can permanently conquer depression by his own might or power; he must rely on God's Holy Spirit for strength and guidance.

# 21

### Trust God

*O wretched man that I am! who shall deliver me from the body of this death?* (Rom. 7:24).

---

Often those people who struggle with emotions that are difficult to handle can identify with this verse. They are confused as to the way out of this emotional entrapment. It is important for them to remember that there is a friend who will help. The victory can be won through Jesus Christ.

# 22

### Trust God

*I can do all things through Christ which strengtheneth me* (Phil. 4:13).

---

Seventy-five percent of people who are significantly depressed feel they will never get better. They are wrong. We can overcome depression through Christ. Sometimes the answers are not simple, but there definitely is hope. This verse of Scripture *proves* that for the Christian there is no such thing as "can't." We *can* do *all things* through Christ who strengthens us. It also shows that we must *participate* with God. He won't make our depression go away automatically, but will give us the *strength* to do what He wants us to do. Passive Christians wait around for God to make their depressions go away without participating with God through responsible action—and then they wonder why they remain depressed for years and years.

# 23

**Trust God**

*Casting all your care upon him; for he careth for you* (I Peter 5:7).

---

The depressed individual may feel that no one cares. God cares and longs for the individual to know that He does. He desires that we turn over our anxieties to Him, believing He will help us. We should let God "worry" about the things we tend to get anxious about, for He won't develop ulcers or depression.

# 24

## Depend on God

*For I know that in me (that is, in my flesh) dwelleth
no good thing; for to will is present with me; but how
to perform that which is good I find not* (Rom. 7:18).

---

A legalistic attitude can add to an already existing
depression. God desires for us to realize that the
Christian life is a supernatural life and can be lived
only through the power of the Holy Spirit.

# 25

## Depend on God

*And he said unto me, My grace is sufficient for thee: for my strength is made perfect in weakness. Most gladly therefore will I rather glory in my infirmities, that the power of Christ may rest upon me*

(II Cor. 12:9).

---

The depressed person often has feelings of inadequacy out of all proportion to reality. He needs to realize that God's strength is "made perfect in weakness." Many Christians become discouraged by what they regard as their uncorrectable defects. They frequently even become angry at God for not making them perfect. In order to keep the apostle Paul humble, God gave him a physical defect (probably an eye disorder). Three different times Paul prayed in faith for God to heal him, but on all three occasions God said no. Paul resolved his inferiority feelings by depending on God to make the right decision, even though that meant he would be left with his infirmity. Paul turned his gloomy attitude to joy, deciding to glory in his infirmities, so the power of Christ could be demonstrated through him.

# PART TWO

## Focusing on Christ

# 26

### Accept Christ as a New Resource

*Therefore if any man be in Christ, he is a new creature: old things are passed away; behold, all things are become new* (II Cor. 5:17).

---

The realization that Christ died for our sins and the acceptance of Him as our Savior can give us a tremendous resource for dealing with problems (including depression). When we accept Christ, we become new in our spirit. The Holy Spirit comes to indwell us. He desires to transform our mind, emotions, and will over a period of time. Acceptance of Christ does not immediately relieve depression, but it gives us a highly effective new resource for dealing with the depression.

# 27

### Learn to Rest in Christ

*Come unto me, all ye that labour and are heavy laden, and I will give you rest. Take my yoke upon you, and learn of me; for I am meek and lowly in heart: and ye shall find rest unto your souls. For my yoke is easy, and my burden is light* (Matt. 11:28-30).

---

One symptom of depression is boredom. The everyday things that one used to enjoy (job, recreation, etc.) become laborious and tiresome. In this verse the depressed person is invited to embark on a supernatural adventure—the adventure of learning from the Scriptures and the Holy Spirit those things which produce the internal rest that only God can give. Many Christians try to cover up their sad emotions by taking on more and more work. They become workaholics to avoid looking at themselves or their true feelings. They fool themselves into thinking these additional responsibilities are from God. Then they get angry at God for giving them such a difficult yoke and such heavy burdens.

In reality, the difficult yoke and heavy burdens are not from God, but are self-imposed. They are a choice, perhaps handed down from perfectionistic, overly-demanding parents or from a legalistic, negativistic church. They may even be a compensation for suppressed inferiority feelings and a fear of failure. God wants us to cast off our self-imposed difficult tasks and heavy burdens and replace them with His easy yoke and light burden. We don't need to waste our time doing twenty superfluous chores a day to prove our worth. It is better to do every day two or three things which God convinces us to do, and to do them well!

# 28

### Enjoy Christ

*For the law of the Spirit of life in Christ Jesus has set you free from the law of sin and of death*
(Rom. 8:2, NASB).

Many of us regard God as a tyrant who puts us on a legalistic treadmill, demanding strict adherence to rigid laws. But God does not want us to be His slaves; rather His Spirit grants us a refreshing freedom. God's principles are His gift of love to us. If we joyfully live according to God's wise recommendations, then we will have love, joy, peace, and the other fruits of the Spirit. But if we self-righteously and legalistically impose on ourselves rigid laws, thinking them to be from God, then we will suffer the consequences of this subtle form of "religious" sin. God wants us to enjoy "the Spirit of life in Christ Jesus," rather than to be bound by "the law of sin and of death."

# PART THREE

# Focusing on God's Word

# 29

## Meditate on God's Word

*This book of the law shall not depart out of thy mouth; but thou shalt meditate therein day and night, that thou mayest observe to do according to all that is written therein: for then thou shalt make thy way prosperous, and then thou shalt have good success* (Josh. 1:8).

---

To gain stability in life, nothing is more helpful than memorizing and meditating on God's Word. God will slowly but surely chip away at problems in our life with His Word.

# 30

### Meditate on God's Word

*But his delight is in the law of the Lord; and in his law doth he meditate day and night. And he shall be like a tree planted by the rivers of water, that bringeth forth his fruit in his season; his leaf also shall not wither; and whatsoever he doeth shall prosper*

(Ps. 1:2, 3).

In these verses we have the picture of a very stable man. We, too, can develop stability by delighting ourselves in God's Word. By meditating on God's Word throughout the day ("day and night") we can be as strong as a tree planted by a river. We will bring forth the fruits of the Spirit—*love, joy* and *peace*—rather than bitterness, depression, and anxiety.

# 31

## Meditate on God's Word

*It is the spirit that quickeneth; the flesh profiteth nothing: the words that I speak unto you, they are spirit, and they are life* (John 6:63).

---

God desires that we spend time in His Word because it gives "life." One way that God's Spirit ministers to our human spirit is through our meditating on God's love letter to us—His Word.

# 32

## Meditate on God's Word

*I have written unto you, fathers, because ye have known him that is from the beginning. I have written unto you, young men, because ye are strong, and the word of God abideth in you, and ye have overcome the wicked one* (I John 2:14).

---

One way the evil one desires to render a Christian in-effective is through depression. The young men referred to in this verse are described as strong. They were strong because the Word of God was in them. The Word of God can also make us strong today and, thus, less prone to depression. We should memorize it, meditate on it, and—most importantly—apply it to our lives.

# 33

## Live by the Counsel of God's Word

*And he said unto them, Set your hearts unto all the words which I testify among you this day, which ye shall command your children to observe to do, all the words of this law. For it is not a vain thing for you; because it is your life* (Deut. 32:46, 47a).

---

The depressed person often despairs of life. God desires that His Word become our very life. As it does, it can help an individual to overcome depression. God also desires that we teach His Word to our children, so they as well can live the abundant life! Depression must be avoided in children as well as adults, and living by God's principles is our chief defense.

# 34

**Live by the Counsels of God's Word**

*Thy testimonies also are my delight and my counselors* (Ps. 119:24).

---

The depressed individual longs for a counselor to help him figure a way out of what he regards as a hopeless situation. God's Word is the best counselor he can have, even though God frequently uses a "multitude of counselors" to help in time of despair.

# 35

**Live by the Counsels of God's Word**

*Therefore, whosoever heareth these sayings of mine, and doeth them, I will liken him unto a wise man, which built his house upon a rock: And the rain descended, and the floods came, and the winds blew, and beat upon that house, and it fell not: for it was founded upon a rock* (Matt. 7:24, 25).

---

Notice that in this verse the rain did descend, the floods did come, and the wind did blow; but the house did not fall. Troubles and problems will come, but by hearing and doing the Word of God we can be stable.

# 36

## Recognize the Supernatural Power of God's Word

*And now, brethren, I commend you to God, and to the word of his grace, which is able to build you up, and to give you an inheritance among all them which are sanctified* (Acts 20:32).

---

Whenever we feel a little down, nothing can lift our mood as can the Word of God. There is something about it that lifts our mood in a supernatural way. The Word of God can actually build us up.

# 37

**Recognize the Supernatural Power of God's Word**

*For this cause also thank we God without ceasing, because, when ye received the word of God which ye heard of us, ye received it not as the word of men, but as it is in truth, the word of God, which effectually worketh also in you that believe* (I Thess. 2:13).

The Word of God is not like the word of men. It is absolutely inerrant and supernatural. It can effectively work in us to overcome our depression.

# 38

## Recognize the Supernatural Power of God's Word

*For the word of God is quick, and powerful, and sharper than any two-edged sword, piercing even to the dividing asunder of soul and spirit, and of the joints and marrow, and is a discerner of the thoughts and intents of the heart* (Heb. 4:12).

---

The Word of God is quick, powerful, and sharp. It can help an individual to overcome depression. It can help us discern which thoughts are of God and which are not. The depressed individual needs to remember that God condemns his sinful behavior but not him. God desires that the depressed individual change his negative, self-derogatory thinking.

# 39

**Recognize the Supernatural Power of God's Word**

*Through faith we understand that the worlds are framed by the word of God, so that things which are seen were not made of things which do appear*

(Heb. 11:3).

God created the whole universe by His spoken word. How powerful His spoken word must be: If one traveled across the Milky Way at the speed of light, he would be 100,000 years old on completing the journey. And the Milky Way is only one of billions of galaxies. If God's spoken word can create a universe, then His written word can overcome depression.

# 40

### Hold Fast to God's Promises

*Wherefore, sirs, be of good cheer: for I believe God, that it shall be even as it was told me* (Acts 27:25).

When the apostle Paul said these words, the ship he was on was about to sink. The crew was experiencing extreme anxiety. Sometimes we need just to be patient and hold fast to the promises of God.

# 41

**Fill Inner Emptiness with the Joys of God's Word**

*The grass withers, the flower fades, But the word of our God stands forever* (Isa. 40:8, NASB).

---

The depressed person feels an emptiness inside. God desires to fill that emptiness with His Word. His Word will "stand forever."

# 42

**Fill Inner Emptiness with the Joys of God's Word**

*Thy words were found, and I did eat them; and thy word was unto me the joy and rejoicing of mine heart: for I am called by thy name, O Lord God of hosts* (Jer. 15:16).

---

The Word of God can literally give us joy that will help to counteract depression. Meditation on Scripture will result in a rejoicing heart.

# 43

**Fill Inner Emptiness with the Joys of God's Word**

*And they said one to another, Did not our heart burn within us, while he talked with us by the way, and while he opened to us the scriptures?*

(Luke 24:32).

The Scriptures are alive. If we regard the Bible as more than just a book to be studied, we will begin to really enjoy it and allow it to encourage us. It can "burn within" our hearts as it brings about healing.

# PART FOUR

## Praying for Help
## and Guidance

# 44

## Be Bold to Call on God

*And Jabez called on the God of Israel, saying, Oh that thou wouldest bless me indeed, and enlarge my coast, and that thine hand might be with me, and that thou wouldest keep me from evil, that it may not grieve me! And God granted him that which he requested* (I Chron. 4:10).

---

Jabez called upon God. He was bold. He asked God to bless him and to keep him from evil (harm). God "granted him that which he requested." Do we dare be as bold as Jabez was? Why not? God certainly seemed pleased with Jabez.

# 45

### Express Your Problems to God

*Evening, and morning, and at noon, will I pray, and cry aloud: and he shall hear my voice* (Ps. 55: 17).

One of the most powerful techniques in psychotherapy is the simple tool of letting the client ventilate. If the ventilation of feelings helps in psychotherapy, how much more does it help to ventilate to God who has supernatural power to change the situation. David cried aloud to God and God heard him.

# 46

### Express Your Problems to God

*And he spake a parable unto them to this end, that men ought always to pray, and not to faint*

(Luke 18:1).

When we are feeling discouraged and about to "faint," God desires that we talk with Him about the situation. This prayer does two things. First, it gets the problem out from inside of us where it would cause depressive feelings. Second, it calls upon God who has supernatural power to deal with the problem.

# 47

### Express Your Problems to God

*Be anxious for nothing, but in everything by prayer and supplication with thanksgiving let your requests be made known to God* (Phil. 4:6, NASB).

One way to conquer anxiety is through prayer. God desires that we express our problems and needs to Him. We should thank Him for everything, including our occasional sufferings, trusting that He will use all our experience as a means for our edification.

# 48

**Be Assured God Will Answer You**

*He shall call upon me, and I will answer him: I will be with him in trouble; I will deliver him, and honour him* (Ps. 91:15).

---

Today, God answers our prayers just as He did those of our forefathers years ago. He is with us in trouble. He will deliver us from our emotional pain.

# 49

## Be Assured God Will Answer You

*Elias was a man subject to like passions as we are, and he prayed earnestly that it might not rain: and it rained not on the earth by the space of three years and six months* (James 5:17).

---

Elijah was a man subject to like passions as we are (including depression—see I Kings 19:4), and yet God honored his prayers. When we are depressed, we feel so worthless that we think God will not honor our prayers; yet He says He will!

# PART FIVE

## Avoiding Satan and Sin

# 50

### Be Aware of the Techniques of Satan

*Simon, Simon, behold, Satan has demanded permission to sift you like wheat; but I have prayed for you, that your faith may not fail; and you, when once you have turned again, strengthen your brothers*
(Luke 22:31, 32, NASB).

---

Satan does desire to have us and render us ineffective by whatever means he can. Of course, depression is an excellent way to render a Christian ineffective. Notice what Christ said. He said that He would protect Peter. Christ encouraged Peter once he "turned again" to help his brothers.

# 51

## Be Aware of the Techniques of Satan

*Finally, my brethren, be strong in the Lord, and in the power of his might. Put on the whole armor of God, that ye may be able to stand against the wiles of the devil. For we wrestle not against flesh and blood, but against principalities, against powers, against the rulers of the darkness of this world, against spiritual wickedness in high places* (Eph. 6:10-12).

---

The devil has many schemes to trip up Christians. We wrestle against evil spiritual forces. I believe one of the major means used by these evil forces on serious Christians is depression. God encourages us to stand firm against these evil forces by putting on the full armor of God—truth (including the truth about ourselves), righteousness (right behavior), the gospel of peace, faith, salvation, the Word of God, and prayer.

# 52

### Resist the Devil

*Submit yourselves therefore to God. Resist the devil, and he will flee from you. Draw nigh to God, and he will draw nigh to you. Cleanse your hands, ye sinners; and purify your hearts, ye double minded*

(James 4:7, 8).

---

Christians cannot be demon-possessed, since God, who is in us, is stronger than the devil, and since I Corinthians 10:13 promises that God always provides to the Christian a way to escape all temptations. However, the devil loves to harass Christians. In James 4:7, 8, God promises that merely resisting the devil will result in his fleeing from us. Many Christians love to blame the devil for their own irresponsible behavior. This temporarily relieves some of their guilt feelings. As Christians, however, we must instead resist the devil and draw nigh to God. The devil will flee and God will quickly draw nigh to us.

# 53

## Avoid Sin

*By faith Moses, when he was come to years, refused to be called the son of Pharaoh's daughter; Choosing rather to suffer affliction with the people of God, than to enjoy the pleasures of sin for a season; Esteeming the reproach of Christ greater riches than the treasures in Egypt: for he had respect unto the recompence of the reward* (Heb. 11:24-26).

---

When individuals are depressed, they may turn to various sins for relief. Little do they realize that their depression will usually be intensified by the resulting guilt. Moses had perspective. He knew there was pleasure in sin, and he also knew the pleasure lasted only for a season.

# 54

## Avoid Sin

*Dearly beloved, I beseech you as strangers and pilgrims, abstain from fleshly lusts, which war against the soul* (I Peter 2:11).

---

Sin has a destructive effect upon the mind, emotions, and will of man. It erodes relationships and generates insecurities which can lead to severe depression and various other psychological problems. Guilt is one form of anger—anger at the self. Pent-up anger is the root cause of the vast majority of severe depressions. Repenting from a specific sin is frequently the major turning point in getting over a guilt-induced depression.

# 55

### Avoid Sin

*Do not love the world, nor the things in the world. If any one loves the world, the love of the Father is not in him. For all that is in the world, the lust of the flesh and the lust of the eyes and the boastful pride of life, is not from the Father, but is from the world*
(I John 2:15, 16, NASB).

---

The person who is depressed should ask himself what he is doing to make himself depressed. He may discover that he is living a life-style that is clearly against God. If that is the case, then he needs to stop doing those things, and ask God to forgive him for his past actions and attitudes. All humans have inferiority feelings, and we tend to compensate for these feelings by yielding to the lust of the flesh (e. g., sexual sins), lust of the eyes (e.g., buying everything in sight), or the pride of life (power struggles or status-seeking behavior). God wants us to accept the fact that in Him we find our own worth, and to quit using these foolish, immature, sinful, and worldly behavior patterns to compensate for false feelings of inferiority. They can result only in an ultimate lowering of self-esteem and an increased rate of depression.

# PART SIX

## Drawing Strength from Others

# 56

## Learn from Others Who Have Been Depressed

*He sent from above, he took me, he drew me out of many waters* (Ps. 18:16).

---

In depression the individual often sees no way out and no hope for the future. God helped King David to have victory over many depressing circumstances. He can help us today to have victory over circumstances and problems.

# 57

**Learn from Others Who Have Been Depressed**

*This I recall to my mind; therefore have I hope. It is of the Lord's mercies that we are not consumed, because his compassions fail not* (Lam. 3:21, 22).

---

Jeremiah, who penned the Book of Lamentations, has been called the weeping prophet. He knew what it is like to feel depressed. He found hope when he came to realize the compassion and faithfulness of God.

# 58

## Learn from Others Who Have Been Depressed

*There hath no temptation taken you but such as is common to man: but God is faithful, who will not suffer you to be tempted above that ye are able; but will with the temptation also make a way to escape, that ye may be able to bear it* (I Cor. 10:13).

Many who have experienced depression state that they have been greatly helped by finding other Christians who have also suffered from depression. They came to realize the depression is "common to man" —even Christians. God has provided ways to escape depression, as well as ways to escape all temptations to sin. Passive Christians frequently fool themselves into thinking they cannot give up a sin or bad habit which leads to depression. This verse proves that they really *can* if they want to, by using God's way of escape. Whenever a Christian finds himself using the word "can't," he should stop and change it to "won't" instead. Then he will see the real truth.

# 59

### Draw Close to Your Mate

*Whoso findeth a wife findeth a good thing, and obtaineth favour of the Lord* (Prov. 18:22).

---

The greatest encouragement in life can be one's mate. The mate listens, accepts, and can help to counteract the sense of failure, the social withdrawal, and the poor self-image that the depressive feels.

# 60

## Develop Friendships

*A friend loveth at all times, and a brother is born for adversity* (Prov. 17:17).

---

Mental health is important to all people. In order to maintain one's mental health, it is necessary to have a sense of being valued by others. Friendships are one of the key ways in which people learn to value others and experience being valued. That is why God encourages us so many times to "love one another."

# 61

## Develop Friendships

*Iron sharpeneth iron; so a man sharpeneth the countenance of his friend* (Prov. 27:17).

---

Research reveals that a majority of individuals who become significantly depressed feel they have no one with whom they are close. Developing a close friendship can be a first step toward becoming well. Close friends will love you enough to confront you when your behavior or motives are improper.

# 62

## Develop Friendships

*Two are better than one; because they have a good reward for their labour. For if they fall, the one will lift up his fellow: but woe to him that is alone when he falleth; for he hath not another to help him up*

(Eccles. 4:9, 10).

---

Friends offer protection against depression. If we are alone in our battles, it is not a matter of *if* we fall but only *when*. God desires that we have a strong support system. Then we can lift each other up when we fall.

# 63

### Develop Friendships

*Nevertheless God, that comforteth those that are cast down, comforted us by the coming of Titus*

(II Cor. 7:6).

---

One way God often chooses to help us when we are feeling down is to bring a Christian friend to us. The apostle Paul was discouraged until Titus came to comfort him.

# 64

## Develop Friendships

*And let us consider one another to provoke unto love and to good works: Not forsaking the assembling of ourselves together, as the manner of some is; but exhorting one another: and so much the more, as ye see the day approaching* (Heb. 10:24, 25).

---

The depressed person wants to withdraw from people and often does. The more he withdraws, the more depressed he gets, and the more depressed he becomes, the more he withdraws, and so the cycle goes. God desires that we do not forsake "the assembling of ourselves together." We need each other. We need to exhort each other. The depressed person must force himself to communicate on an intense personal level with godly friends if he wants to recover.

# 65

### Help Others

*Blessed be God, even the Father of our Lord Jesus Christ, the Father of mercies, and the God of all comfort; Who comforteth us in all our tribulation, that we may be able to comfort them which are in any trouble, by the comfort wherewith we ourselves are comforted of God* (II Cor. 1:3, 4).

---

As God comforts us in our tribulations, we need to comfort and help others. In fact, an individual that is depressed can help to relieve his own depression by getting out and helping someone else.

# 66

## Help Others

*Let each of you look not only to his own interests, but also to the interests of others* (Phil. 2:4, RSV).

As we become more involved in helping others (spiritually—sharing Bible verses with them; psychologically—counseling with them; and physically—helping them with a chore), we become less wrapped up in our own problems, and our mental state actually improves.

# 67

## Help Others

*For God is not unrighteous to forget your work and labour of love, which ye have shewed toward his name, in that ye have ministered to the saints, and do minister* (Heb. 6:10).

---

Sincere Christians may become depressed from time to time, feeling that their labor is in vain. God has promised that He will not forget when we minister to fellow Christians. He will reward us richly for it.

# PART SEVEN

## Dealing with Faulty
## Individual Life Patterns

# 68

## Change Thought Patterns

*And be not conformed to this world: but be ye transformed by the renewing of your mind, that ye may prove what is that good, and acceptable, and perfect, will of God* (Rom. 12:2).

---

Our brains operate like computers. Often they have a lot of negative programing from the past. God desires that we reprogram our minds into His positive ways of thinking.

# 69

### Change Thought Patterns

*Finally, brethren, whatsoever things are true, whatsoever things are honest, whatsoever things are just, whatsoever things are pure, whatsoever things are lovely, whatsoever things are of good report; if there be any virtue, and if there be any praise, think on these things* (Phil. 4:8).

---

While depression causes painful (negative) thinking, it is also true that negative thinking in turn reinforces the depression. One way to overcome depression is by being careful to think on positive things as much as possible.

# 70

## Realize There Is Hope

*For David speaketh concerning him, I foresaw the Lord always before my face, for he is on my right hand, that I should not be moved: Therefore did my heart rejoice, and my tongue was glad; moreover also my flesh shall rest in hope* (Acts 2: 25, 26).

---

In depression a feeling of hopelessness and a lack of stability often exist. David found stability and hope through a close walk with God. David's hope in God brought freedom from anxiety (rest) to his flesh.

# 71

**Understand Feelings**

*Cast not away therefore your confidence, which hath great recompence of reward. For ye have need of patience, that, after ye have done the will of God, ye might receive the promise* (Heb. 10:35, 36).

---

An individual who is depressed tends to lose his confidence and feel that everything is hopeless and that he is helpless. God has encouraged us not to throw away our confidence. With God at our side, the situation is not hopeless, and we are not helpless.

# 72

## Focus on Behavior

*Then the Lord said to Cain, "Why are you angry? And why has your countenance fallen? If you do well, will not your countenance be lifted up? And if you do not do well, sin is crouching at the door; and its desire is for you, but you must master it"*

(Gen 4:6, 7, NASB).

---

As an individual becomes depressed he tends to focus on how he feels. And while feelings certainly are important (they should be talked out and understood), an individual should be careful that he doesn't let them force him to withdraw. Involvement in wholesome activities and behavior can help to change his bad feelings. Behavior precedes feelings. God told Cain that if he would *do* right, he would end up *feeling* right. The same principle applies to us today.

# 73

**Focus on Behavior**

*Wherefore seeing we also are compassed about with so great a cloud of witnesses, let us lay aside every weight, and the sin which doth so easily beset us, and let us run with patience the race that is set before us, Looking unto Jesus, the author and finisher of our faith; who for the joy that was set before him endured the cross, despising the shame, and is set down at the right hand of the throne of God. For consider him that endured such contradiction of sinners against himself, lest ye be wearied and faint in your minds* (Heb. 12:1-3).

---

Depression is like a weight around the neck. God desires that we lay this weight aside. I believe that running the race for Christ helps us to continue to lay the weight of depression aside. Considering what Christ went through helps us not to faint in our minds.

# 74

### Focus on Behavior

*As every man hath received the gift, even so minister the same one to another, as good stewards of the manifold grace of God* (I Peter 4:10).

---

According to this verse, each person has something to give to others. The depressed person is helped when he stops focusing on his sad feelings and begins to do things with and for others. This will be difficult to do at first, but it will eventually help to lift the depression.

# 75

## Focus on the Present

*Brethren, I do not regard myself as having laid hold of it yet, but one thing I do: forgetting what lies behind and reaching forward to what lies ahead, I press on toward the goal for the prize of the upward call of God in Christ Jesus* (Phil. 3:13, 14, NASB).

---

The depressed individual often ruminates over the past—past sins and past mistakes. The future looks dim. He needs to learn to forget the past, to live in the present, and to look forward to the future. He must not hold grudges against himself, God, or others for any past events. He must turn all vengeance over to God, since that is God's business. He must forgive and forget, once he has dealt adequately with any past conflict.

# 76

**Deal with Guilt**

*When I kept silence, my bones waxed old through my roaring all the day long* (Ps. 32:3).

---

Guilt is often a major factor in depression. King David found relief from his guilt and subsequent depression by confessing his sins to God.

# 77

## Deal with Guilt

*As far as the east is from the west, so far hath he removed our transgressions from us. Like as a father pitieth his children, so the Lord pitieth them that fear him. For he knoweth our frame; he remembereth that we are dust* (Ps. 103:12-14).

---

The depressed individual's thinking is often permeated with guilt (true and false). He has a very difficult time forgiving himself. Learning to deal with his guilt can be of much benefit. God says that He removes our sins as far as the east is from the west. He is also empathetic toward us—He knows we are but dust.

# 78

### Deal with Guilt

*And herein do I exercise myself, to have always a conscience void of offence toward God, and toward men* (Acts 24:16).

---

Guilt resulting from a wrong committed against a friend can be a cause of depression. Working on developing a clear conscience toward the one offended can help in relieving this depression.

# 79

## Deal with Guilt

*If we confess our sins, he is faithful and just to forgive us our sins, and to cleanse us from all unrighteousness* (I John 1:9).

---

Research has emphasized that guilt is a major contributing factor to depression. Self-punishment by dwelling on one's guilt is not a part of God's plan for us. We need to give up our guilts to God and allow Him to fulfill His role as our Father by ministering to our hurts. Holding a grudge against ourselves for an already confessed sin is a worse sin than that for which we feel guilty. It is a rejection of God's offer of total grace and forgiveness.

# 80

## Deal with Guilt

*But whoever has the world's goods, and beholds his brother in need and closes his heart against him, how does the love of God abide in him? Little children, let us not love with word or with tongue, but in deed and truth. We shall know by this that we are of the truth, and shall assure our heart before Him, in whatever our heart condemns us; for God is greater than our heart, and knows all things*

(I John 3:17-20, NASB).

---

False guilt is often present in depression. In fact, guilt usually permeates the thinking of a depressed individual. The heart is often self-condemning. God desires for us to realize that false guilt is just that—false. He desires to relieve us of false guilt. People who were reared by overly-strict, demanding, and critical parents usually feel guilty for ridiculous things that God in no way condemns.

# 81

## Deal with Anger

*You shall not hate your fellow-countryman in your heart; you may surely reprove your neighbor, but shall not incur sin because of him. You shall not take vengeance, nor bear any grudge against the sons of your people, but you shall love your neighbor as yourself; I am the Lord* (Lev. 19:17, 18, NASB).

---

This verse shows us that it is very appropriate for us to tactfully reprove a neighbor or friend who offends us. But we must never hold any grudges or seek vengeance. Vengeance is God's business; it is not our business. The only unconscious motive there is for holding a grudge for any past offense is a subtle desire to get vengeance on the person who offended us. Holding grudges and a vengeful attitude are the primary root causes of depression, and they are both sin. If we would only realize that getting angry is normal and reproving the person who offends us (before bedtime, according to Ephesians 4:26) is godly and even commanded, it would be much easier for us to forgive people who offend us and we might even help them change their offensive behavior as well.

# 82

### Deal with Anger

*Be angry, and yet do not sin; do not let the sun go down on your anger* (Eph. 4:26, NASB).

---

The apostle Paul tells us that we can get angry without sinning, but that we should never let the sun go down on our wrath (that is, we should never hold grudges past bedtime). In other words, it is all right to get angry when we suffer a significant loss or when someone sins against us. Anger is an automatic human response. But somehow, with God's help, we must by bedtime forgive whomever we feel anger toward, whether they deserve forgiveness or not. God wants us to forgive others *and ourselves* for our own good because if we hold grudges, we will eventually become clinically depressed.

# 83

### Deal with Anger

*Let all bitterness, and wrath, and anger, and clamour, and evil speaking, be put away from you, with all malice: And be ye kind one to another, tenderhearted, forgiving one another, even as God for Christ's sake hath forgiven you* (Eph. 4:31, 32).

A person who holds a grudge or is hostile toward another person often reaps negative physical and psychological reactions because of the emotional stress he places on his own body. This verse encourages us to take away such destructive attitudes. Furthermore, it challenges us to practice positive wholesome attitudes and behaviors toward others.

# 84

**Deal with Anger**

*Wherefore, my beloved brethren, let every man be swift to hear, slow to speak, slow to wrath: For the wrath of man worketh not the righteousness of God* (James 1:19, 20).

---

Many of us live in a demanding, high-tension world. Rapid decision-making often is a necessity. The results of this life-style are at times emotionally draining. Yet, God challenges us to be the kind of people who take the time to be understanding of others and respond to them in a sensible manner. We should be slow to speak (a good listener) and slow to wrath (patient). We can be slow to wrath by giving up some of our selfish desires and unrealistic expectations.

# 85

## Realize God's Ability

*The horse is prepared for the day of battle, but victory belongs to the Lord* (Prov. 21:31, NASB).

---

There are two perspectives in this verse: individual responsibility and God's sovereignty. In times of mental stress we need to be responsible (do what we can to deal with the problem) but we also need to realize that God controls everything. Relax and be comforted because the victory belongs to Him.

# 86

## Deal with Fear

*I sought the Lord, and he heard me, and delivered me from all my fears* (Ps. 34:4).

In depression there are many fears. Over 350 times in the Scriptures we are told to fear not. God desires to help us overcome our fears by seeking him.

# 87

### Deal with Fear

*What time I am afraid, I will trust in thee* (Ps. 56:3).

---

By trusting God, David found peace from his fears when he was in a difficult situation. We can do the same today.

# 88

### Deal with Fear

*Fear thou not; for I am with thee: be not dismayed; for I am thy God: I will strengthen thee; yea, I will help thee; yea, I will uphold thee with the right hand of my righteousness* (Isa. 41:10).

---

In today's fast-paced, mobile society, there are many threats to our emotional stability. Still, the same God who ages ago comforted and supported His children with the fact of His presence continues to comfort and support His children today in the same way. He will uphold us with His strong right hand.

# 89

### Deal with Fear

*Peace I leave with you, my peace I give unto you: not as the world giveth, give I unto you. Let not your heart be troubled, neither let it be afraid* (John 14:27).

---

The depressed person's heart is filled with trouble. He has feelings of sadness, helplessness, hopelessness, worthlessness, and loneliness. He has guilt, worry, and a negative self-concept. God desires to give peace to comfort this troubled heart with its many fears.

# 90

## Deal with Fear

*There is no fear in love; but perfect love casts out fear*
(I John 4;18a, NASB).

---

Depressed individuals often intensely fear rejection by their friends. God wants us to know how much He loves us. A realization of this love will cast out fear. He will never reject us (Hebrews 13:5).

# 91

## Deal with Fears of Rejection

*For my father and my mother have forsaken me, But the Lord will take me up* (Ps. 27:10, NASB).

A lack of closeness with father and mother can result in unmet dependency needs, fears of rejection, a resistance to getting close to others, and many of the other symptoms of depression. In this verse, God speaks to those who have been forsaken by their father and mother and says that He will take them up.

# 92

## Deal with Fears of Rejection

*Let your conversation [manner of life] be without covetousness; and be content with such things as ye have; for he hath said, I will never leave thee, nor forsake thee* (Heb. 13:5).

---

The depressed person intensely fears rejection by others. In fact, he feels that he is a nobody and deserves rejection. God has assured His children that they are of great worth to Him and the He will never reject them.

# 93

### Deal with Worry

*Therefore do not be anxious for tomorrow; for tomorrow will care for itself. Each day has enough trouble of its own* (Matt. 6:34, NASB).

---

We can prevent much worry by learning to live one day at a time. Probably ninety-eight percent of what we worry about will never come true. God tells us in this verse that todays conflicts are enough to cope with—we must not be anxious over tomorrow's potential hazards, most of which will never happen.

# 94

### Deal with Worry

*And that which fell among thorns are they, which, when they have heard, go forth, and are choked with cares and riches and pleasures of this life, and bring no fruit to perfection* (Luke 8:14).

---

In this verse three things are listed that can "choke" persons after they have heard the Word of God. Many of us have often heard sermons on two of these —riches and pleasures of this life. And yet, worries (cares or anxieties) are also listed. A major step in overcoming depression is to learn to deal with worry and anxiety.

# 95

### Deal with Worry

*We are troubled on every side, yet not distressed; we are perplexed, but not in despair; Persecuted, but not forsaken; cast down, but not destroyed*

(II Cor. 4:8, 9).

---

There is nothing wrong with being perplexed, but it is wrong to carry this to despair. Being perplexed drives us to Christ, but remaining in despair results in depression.

# 96

## Deal with Weakness

*For we do not have a high priest who cannot sympathize with our weaknesses, but one who has been tempted in all things as we are, yet without sin*
(Heb. 4:15, NASB).

---

A person can become depressed because he is faced with a temptation that is extremely hard for him to handle. Christ as a man fully felt and successfully dealt with personal temptations. Now, as our High Priest, Christ can be a strength to us and, when needed, forgiving to us. He understands what we are going through.

### Deal with Situational Problems

*And we know that all things work together for good to them that love God, to them who are the called according to his purpose* (Rom. 8:28).

---

In the early 1970s, Holmes and Rahe developed a chart assigning "life change units" to various situational changes and problems (death of relative, illness, retirement, financial problems, job changes, change in residence, etc.). They found that an accumulation of 200 or more units in a single year results in a significant increase in psychiatric problems (such as depression). This verse can be a tremendous comfort to God's children when they are going through situational problems. God promises to make all of our situational problems work together for good in the long run. This does not mean that God *directs* all of our situational problems, as some Christians erroneously suppose. God *may* direct some of them, and we *can* be assured that no situational problem comes our way without God's *permitting* it. Moreover, no situational problem will ever come our way without God's being intimately involved in our lives. In every situational problem, whether God directs it or permits it, God will teach us lessons that will benefit us greatly in the long run. Christians bring a great many situational problems on themselves, either consciously or subconsciously, but God will make even our self-imposed situational problems work together for good.

# 98

## Develop Patience

*But the God of all grace, who hath called us unto his eternal glory by Christ Jesus, after that ye have suffered a while, make you perfect, stablish, strengthen, settle you* (I Peter 5:10).

---

God can use the difficult times in our lives to make us strong. In fact, the difficult times in our own lives can make us more empathetic with others. In this passage God promises to strengthen us after we have suffered awhile. God seldom relieves a Christian's severe depression overnight. It may take days, weeks, or even months, depending largely on our degree of cooperation with Him, but also on other factors. There are many valuable lessons to learn through this period of suffering, lessons which will make the depressed individual stronger than he ever was before. By suffering awhile, he will understand the pain of others and be especially able to help them.

# 99

## Be Assertive

*Ask, and it shall be given to you; seek, and you shall find; knock, and it shall be opened to you. For every one who asks receives; and he who seeks finds; and to him who knocks it shall be opened*

(Matt. 7:7, 8, NASB).

---

Almost everyone, including God, can appreciate the person who is straightforward. We don't have to guess what that person wants from us or life or others. We hear him asking, see him seeking, and observe him knocking. The depressed person can greatly benefit by practicing such direct, positive behavior towards others. He should avoid the extremes of being overly passive or overly aggressive, rather he should be *assertive*. He should tell God, his mate, and close friends the truth about his feelings and be assertive with his reasonable requests.

# 100

## Get Sufficient Rest

*But he [Elijah] himself went a day's journey into the wilderness, and came and sat down under a juniper tree: and he requested for himself that he might die; and said, It is enough; now, O Lord, take away my life; for I am not better than my fathers. And as he lay and slept under a juniper tree, behold, then an angel touched him, and said unto him, Arise and eat. And he looked, and behold, there was a cake baken on the coals, and a cruse of water at his head. And he did eat and drink, and laid him down again. And the angel of the Lord came again the second time, and touched him, and said, Arise and eat; because the journey is too great for thee. And he arose, and did eat and drink, and went in the strength of that meat forty days and forty nights unto Horeb the mount of God* (I Kings 19:4-8).

---

In depression, thinking may become very painful—even suicidal. Elijah was a godly man that had been under both emotional and physical stress. He became so depressed he wanted to die. God simply let him get some rest, then gave him something to eat, then let him have more sleep, and once again let him eat. After this simple procedure, Elijah was ready to go again. A good night's sleep can often help when one is upset.